Date _____ Address _____

Name _____

School _____

Grade/Form/Year and Age _____

When I started playing football _____

Who taught me football first _____

Now I play at _____

My coach is _____

Who assist coach _____

My coach calls me _____

Why I like my coach _____

_____

_____

_____

My coach often tells me _____

_____

_____

_____

My coach often tells me _____

_____

_____

Why I like playing football _____

_____

_____

_____

My goal is _____

_____

_____

_____

My favorite teams: 1. _____
2. _____
3. _____

My favorite players: ①. _____
②. _____
③. _____

Three things I admire most about each favorite player

①. -- _____
-- _____
-- _____

②. -- _____
-- _____
-- _____

③. -- _____
-- _____
_____

The interesting things about football _____
_____
_____
_____

The funny thing ever happened to me playing football _____
_____
_____
_____

The bad/weird thing ever happened to me playing football _____
_____
_____
_____

PRE-SEASON PRACTICE

From Monday _____ to Friday _____ How many times _____
            Date   Date

1st practice was: Very easy ☐ Easy ☐ Average ☐ Hard ☐ Very hard ☐

2nd practice was: Very easy ☐ Easy ☐ Average ☐ Hard ☐ Very hard ☐

3rd practice was: Very easy ☐ Easy ☐ Average ☐ Hard ☐ Very hard ☐

1st practice: 🙂 😐 🙁   2nd practice: 🙂 😐 🙁   3rd practice: 🙂 😐 🙁

Coach focused on _____

_____

_____

_____

I focused on _____

_____

_____

What I'v learnt _____

_____

_____

My weaknesses/strengths _____

_____

_____

Coach advice _____

_____

_____

Additional notes _____

_____

_____

PRE-SEASON PRACTICE

From Monday _____ to Friday _____ How many times _____
　　　　　　　　 Date　　　　　　　　　　 Date

1st practice was: Very easy ☐ Easy ☐ Average ☐ Hard ☐ Very hard ☐

2nd practice was: Very easy ☐ Easy ☐ Average ☐ Hard ☐ Very hard ☐

3rd practice was: Very easy ☐ Easy ☐ Average ☐ Hard ☐ Very hard ☐

1st practice: ☺ 😐 ☹　2nd practice: ☺ 😐 ☹　3rd practice: ☺ 😐 ☹

Coach focused on _____

_____

_____

_____

I focused on _____

_____

_____

What I'v learnt _____

_____

_____

My weaknesses/strengths _____

_____

_____

Coach advice _____

_____

_____

Additional notes _____

_____

PRE-SEASON PRACTICE

From Monday _____ to Friday _____ How many times _____
                  Date   Date

1st practice was: Very easy ☐ Easy ☐ Average ☐ Hard ☐ Very hard ☐

2nd practice was: Very easy ☐ Easy ☐ Average ☐ Hard ☐ Very hard ☐

3rd practice was: Very easy ☐ Easy ☐ Average ☐ Hard ☐ Very hard ☐

1st practice: 🙂 😐 🙁 2nd practice: 🙂 😐 🙁 3rd practice: 🙂 😐 🙁

Coach focused on _____

_____

_____

_____

I focused on _____

_____

_____

_____

What I'v learnt _____

_____

_____

_____

My weaknesses/strengths _____

_____

_____

Coach advice _____

_____

_____

_____

Additional notes _____

_____

_____

PRE-SEASON PRACTICE

From Monday _____ to Friday _____ How many times _____
Date   Date

1st practice was: Very easy ☐ Easy ☐ Average ☐ Hard ☐ Very hard ☐

2nd practice was: Very easy ☐ Easy ☐ Average ☐ Hard ☐ Very hard ☐

3rd practice was: Very easy ☐ Easy ☐ Average ☐ Hard ☐ Very hard ☐

1st practice: 🙂 😐 🙁 2nd practice: 🙂 😐 🙁 3rd practice: 🙂 😐 🙁

Coach focused on _____
_____
_____
_____

I focused on _____
_____
_____

What I'v learnt _____
_____
_____

My weaknesses/strengths _____
_____
_____

Coach advice _____
_____
_____

Additional notes _____
_____

PRACTICE

From Monday _____ to Friday _____ How many times ___
            Date   Date

next game _____ How many times ___
                   Date

1st practice was: Very easy ☐ Easy ☐ Average ☐ Hard ☐ Very hard ☐

2nd practice was: Very easy ☐ Easy ☐ Average ☐ Hard ☐ Very hard ☐

3rd practice was: Very easy ☐ Easy ☐ Average ☐ Hard ☐ Very hard ☐

1st practice: 🙂 😐 🙁   2nd practice: 🙂 😐 🙁   3rd practice: 🙂 😐 🙁

Coach focused on
_____
_____
_____

I focused on
_____
_____
_____

What I'v learnt
_____
_____

My weaknesses/strengths
_____
_____

Coach advice
_____
_____
_____

Additional notes
_____
_____

PRACTICE

From Monday _____ to ⟨ Friday _____   How many times ___
                Date   Date
                     next game _____   How many times ___
                                 Date

1st practice was: Very easy ☐ Easy ☐ Average ☐ Hard ☐ Very hard ☐

2nd practice was: Very easy ☐ Easy ☐ Average ☐ Hard ☐ Very hard ☐

3rd practice was: Very easy ☐ Easy ☐ Average ☐ Hard ☐ Very hard ☐

1st practice: ☺ 😐 ☹   2nd practice: ☺ 😐 ☹   3rd practice: ☺ 😐 ☹

Coach focused on
_____
_____
_____

I focused on
_____
_____
_____

What I'v learnt
_____
_____
_____

My weaknesses/strengths
_____
_____

Coach advice
_____
_____
_____

Additional notes
_____
_____
_____

PRACTICE

From Monday _____ to Friday _____ How many times ___
                Date   next game _____ How many times ___
                                      Date

1st practice was: Very easy ☐ Easy ☐ Average ☐ Hard ☐ Very hard ☐
2nd practice was: Very easy ☐ Easy ☐ Average ☐ Hard ☐ Very hard ☐
3rd practice was: Very easy ☐ Easy ☐ Average ☐ Hard ☐ Very hard ☐

1st practice: ☺ 😐 ☹   2nd practice: ☺ 😐 ☹   3rd practice: ☺ 😐 ☹

Coach focused on
_____
_____
_____
_____

I focused on
_____
_____
_____

What I'v learnt
_____
_____
_____

My weaknesses/strengths
_____
_____
_____

Coach advice
_____
_____
_____

Additional notes
_____
_____
_____

PRACTICE

From Monday _____ to ⟨ Friday _____   How many times ___
Date   next game _____   How many times ___
                          Date   Date

1st practice was: Very easy ☐ Easy ☐ Average ☐ Hard ☐ Very hard ☐
2nd practice was: Very easy ☐ Easy ☐ Average ☐ Hard ☐ Very hard ☐
3rd practice was: Very easy ☐ Easy ☐ Average ☐ Hard ☐ Very hard ☐

1st practice: ☺ 😐 ☹   2nd practice: ☺ 😐 ☹   3rd practice: ☺ 😐 ☹

Coach focused on
_____
_____
_____
_____

I focused on
_____
_____
_____

What I'v learnt
_____
_____
_____

My weaknesses/strengths
_____
_____
_____

Coach advice
_____
_____
_____

Additional notes
_____
_____

PRACTICE

From Monday _____ to ⟨ Friday _____   How many times ___
              Date   Date
                      next game _____   How many times ___
                                 Date

1st practice was: Very easy ☐ Easy ☐ Average ☐ Hard ☐ Very hard ☐

2nd practice was: Very easy ☐ Easy ☐ Average ☐ Hard ☐ Very hard ☐

3rd practice was: Very easy ☐ Easy ☐ Average ☐ Hard ☐ Very hard ☐

1st practice: ☺ 😐 ☹ 2nd practice: ☺ 😐 ☹ 3rd practice: ☺ 😐 ☹

Coach focused on
_____
_____
_____

I focused on
_____
_____
_____

What I'v learnt
_____
_____
_____

My weaknesses/strengths
_____
_____

Coach advice
_____
_____
_____

Additional notes
_____
_____

PRACTICE

From Monday _____ to Friday _____ How many times ___
Date   next game _____ How many times ___
             Date   Date

1st practice was: Very easy ☐ Easy ☐ Average ☐ Hard ☐ Very hard ☐
2nd practice was: Very easy ☐ Easy ☐ Average ☐ Hard ☐ Very hard ☐
3rd practice was: Very easy ☐ Easy ☐ Average ☐ Hard ☐ Very hard ☐

1st practice: 🙂 😐 🙁   2nd practice: 🙂 😐 🙁   3rd practice: 🙂 😐 🙁

Coach focused on
_____
_____
_____

I focused on
_____
_____
_____

What I'v learnt
_____
_____
_____

My weaknesses/strengths
_____
_____
_____

Coach advice
_____
_____
_____

Additional notes
_____
_____
_____

PRACTICE

From Monday _____ to < Friday _____ How many times ___
                            Date   Date
                         next game _____ How many times ___
                                      Date

1st practice was: Very easy ☐ Easy ☐ Average ☐ Hard ☐ Very hard ☐

2nd practice was: Very easy ☐ Easy ☐ Average ☐ Hard ☐ Very hard ☐

3rd practice was: Very easy ☐ Easy ☐ Average ☐ Hard ☐ Very hard ☐

1st practice: ☺ 😐 ☹   2nd practice: ☺ 😐 ☹   3rd practice: ☺ 😐 ☹

Coach focused on
_____
_____
_____

I focused on
_____
_____

What I'v learnt
_____
_____

My weaknesses/strengths
_____
_____

Coach advice
_____
_____

Additional notes
_____
_____

PRACTICE

From Monday _____ to < Friday _____ How many times ___
                 Date   next game _____ How many times ___
                                    Date

1st practice was: Very easy ☐ Easy ☐ Average ☐ Hard ☐ Very hard ☐
2nd practice was: Very easy ☐ Easy ☐ Average ☐ Hard ☐ Very hard ☐
3rd practice was: Very easy ☐ Easy ☐ Average ☐ Hard ☐ Very hard ☐

1st practice: ☺ 😐 ☹   2nd practice: ☺ 😐 ☹   3rd practice: ☺ 😐 ☹

Coach focused on
_____
_____
_____

I focused on
_____
_____
_____

What I'v learnt
_____
_____
_____

My weaknesses/strengths
_____
_____
_____

Coach advice
_____
_____
_____

Additional notes
_____
_____
_____

PRACTICE

From Monday _____ to < Friday _____ How many times __
                  Date   Date
                       next game _____ How many times __
                                     Date

1st practice was: Very easy ☐ Easy ☐ Average ☐ Hard ☐ Very hard ☐
2nd practice was: Very easy ☐ Easy ☐ Average ☐ Hard ☐ Very hard ☐
3rd practice was: Very easy ☐ Easy ☐ Average ☐ Hard ☐ Very hard ☐

1st practice: 🙂 😐 🙁 2nd practice: 🙂 😐 🙁 3rd practice: 🙂 😐 🙁

Coach focused on
_____
_____
_____

I focused on
_____
_____
_____

What I'v learnt
_____
_____
_____

My weaknesses/strengths
_____
_____
_____

Coach advice
_____
_____
_____

Additional notes
_____
_____

PRACTICE

From Monday _____ to — Friday _____ How many times ___
                Date   Date
                      — next game _____ How many times ___
                             Date

1st practice was: Very easy ☐ Easy ☐ Average ☐ Hard ☐ Very hard ☐

2nd practice was: Very easy ☐ Easy ☐ Average ☐ Hard ☐ Very hard ☐

3rd practice was: Very easy ☐ Easy ☐ Average ☐ Hard ☐ Very hard ☐

1st practice: 🙂 😑 🙁   2nd practice: 🙂 😑 🙁   3rd practice: 🙂 😑 🙁

Coach focused on
_____
_____
_____
_____

I focused on
_____
_____
_____

What I'v learnt
_____
_____
_____

My weaknesses/strengths
_____
_____
_____

Coach advice
_____
_____
_____

Additional notes
_____
_____

PRACTICE

From Monday _____ to < Friday _____ How many times ___
Date   Date
                next game _____ How many times ___
                         Date

1st practice was: Very easy ☐ Easy ☐ Average ☐ Hard ☐ Very hard ☐

2nd practice was: Very easy ☐ Easy ☐ Average ☐ Hard ☐ Very hard ☐

3rd practice was: Very easy ☐ Easy ☐ Average ☐ Hard ☐ Very hard ☐

1st practice: ☺ 😐 ☹   2nd practice: ☺ 😐 ☹   3rd practice: ☺ 😐 ☹

Coach focused on
_____
_____
_____

I focused on
_____
_____
_____

What I'v learnt
_____
_____

My weaknesses/strengths
_____
_____

Coach advice
_____
_____
_____

Additional notes
_____
_____

PRACTICE

From Monday _____ to ⟨ Friday _____ How many times ___
Date   next game _____ How many times ___
                                        Date
                          Date

1st practice was: Very easy ☐ Easy ☐ Average ☐ Hard ☐ Very hard ☐
2nd practice was: Very easy ☐ Easy ☐ Average ☐ Hard ☐ Very hard ☐
3rd practice was: Very easy ☐ Easy ☐ Average ☐ Hard ☐ Very hard ☐

1st practice: ☺ 😐 ☹ 2nd practice: ☺ 😐 ☹ 3rd practice: ☺ 😐 ☹

Coach focused on
_____
_____
_____

I focused on
_____
_____
_____

What I'v learnt
_____
_____
_____

My weaknesses/strengths
_____
_____
_____

Coach advice
_____
_____
_____

Additional notes
_____
_____

PRACTICE

From Monday _____ to < Friday _____ How many times ___
Date   Date
                          next game _____ How many times ___
                                   Date

1st practice was: Very easy ☐ Easy ☐ Average ☐ Hard ☐ Very hard ☐
2nd practice was: Very easy ☐ Easy ☐ Average ☐ Hard ☐ Very hard ☐
3rd practice was: Very easy ☐ Easy ☐ Average ☐ Hard ☐ Very hard ☐

1st practice: 🙂 😐 🙁   2nd practice: 🙂 😐 🙁   3rd practice: 🙂 😐 🙁

Coach focused on
_____
_____
_____

I focused on
_____
_____
_____

What I'v learnt
_____
_____
_____

My weaknesses/strengths
_____
_____
_____

Coach advice
_____
_____
_____

Additional notes
_____
_____

PRACTICE

From Monday _____ to Friday _____ How many times ___
                               Date   next game _____ How many times ___
                                                    Date

1st practice was: Very easy ☐ Easy ☐ Average ☐ Hard ☐ Very hard ☐
2nd practice was: Very easy ☐ Easy ☐ Average ☐ Hard ☐ Very hard ☐
3rd practice was: Very easy ☐ Easy ☐ Average ☐ Hard ☐ Very hard ☐

1st practice: 🙂 😐 🙁 2nd practice: 🙂 😐 🙁 3rd practice: 🙂 😐 🙁

Coach focused on
_____
_____
_____

I focused on
_____
_____
_____

What I'v learnt
_____
_____
_____

My weaknesses/strengths
_____
_____
_____

Coach advice
_____
_____
_____

Additional notes
_____
_____

PRACTICE

From Monday _____ to ⎨ Friday _____   How many times ___
Date   Date
                         next game _____   How many times ___
                                        Date

1st practice was: Very easy ☐ Easy ☐ Average ☐ Hard ☐ Very hard ☐
2nd practice was: Very easy ☐ Easy ☐ Average ☐ Hard ☐ Very hard ☐
3rd practice was: Very easy ☐ Easy ☐ Average ☐ Hard ☐ Very hard ☐

1st practice: 🙂 😐 🙁   2nd practice: 🙂 😐 🙁   3rd practice: 🙂 😐 🙁

Coach focused on
_____
_____
_____

I focused on
_____
_____
_____

What I'v learnt
_____
_____
_____

My weaknesses/strengths
_____
_____
_____

Coach advice
_____
_____
_____

Additional notes
_____
_____

PRACTICE

From Monday _____ to ⟨ Friday _____   How many times ___
              Date   next game _____   How many times ___
                                        Date
                         Date

1st practice was: Very easy ☐ Easy ☐ Average ☐ Hard ☐ Very hard ☐
2nd practice was: Very easy ☐ Easy ☐ Average ☐ Hard ☐ Very hard ☐
3rd practice was: Very easy ☐ Easy ☐ Average ☐ Hard ☐ Very hard ☐

1st practice: 😊 😐 ☹   2nd practice: 😊 😐 ☹   3rd practice: 😊 😐 ☹

Coach focused on
_____
_____
_____

I focused on
_____
_____
_____

What I'v learnt
_____
_____
_____

My weaknesses/strengths
_____
_____
_____

Coach advice
_____
_____
_____

Additional notes
_____
_____
_____

PRACTICE

From Monday _____ to < Friday _____ How many times __
                    Date   Date
                      next game _____ How many times __
                                  Date

1st practice was: Very easy ☐ Easy ☐ Average ☐ Hard ☐ Very hard ☐
2nd practice was: Very easy ☐ Easy ☐ Average ☐ Hard ☐ Very hard ☐
3rd practice was: Very easy ☐ Easy ☐ Average ☐ Hard ☐ Very hard ☐

1st practice: 🙂 😐 🙁   2nd practice: 🙂 😐 🙁   3rd practice: 🙂 😐 🙁

Coach focused on
_____
_____
_____

I focused on
_____
_____
_____

What I'v learnt
_____
_____
_____

My weaknesses/strengths
_____
_____
_____

Coach advice
_____
_____
_____

Additional notes
_____
_____

PRACTICE

From Monday _____ to ⟨ Friday _____ How many times ___
Date   next game _____ How many times ___
                              Date

1st practice was: Very easy ☐ Easy ☐ Average ☐ Hard ☐ Very hard ☐
2nd practice was: Very easy ☐ Easy ☐ Average ☐ Hard ☐ Very hard ☐
3rd practice was: Very easy ☐ Easy ☐ Average ☐ Hard ☐ Very hard ☐

1st practice: ☺ 😐 ☹   2nd practice: ☺ 😐 ☹   3rd practice: ☺ 😐 ☹

Coach focused on
_____
_____
_____

I focused on
_____
_____
_____

What I'v learnt
_____
_____
_____

My weaknesses/strengths
_____
_____
_____

Coach advice
_____
_____
_____

Additional notes
_____
_____

PRACTICE

From Monday _____ to ⟨ Friday _____   How many times __
Date   next game _____   How many times __
Date

1ˢᵗ practice was: Very easy ☐   Easy ☐   Average ☐   Hard ☐   Very hard ☐

2ⁿᵈ practice was: Very easy ☐   Easy ☐   Average ☐   Hard ☐   Very hard ☐

3ʳᵈ practice was: Very easy ☐   Easy ☐   Average ☐   Hard ☐   Very hard ☐

1ˢᵗ practice: ☺ 😐 ☹   2ⁿᵈ practice: ☺ 😐 ☹   3ʳᵈ practice: ☺ 😐 ☹

Coach focused on
_____
_____
_____

I focused on
_____
_____

What I'v learnt
_____
_____
_____

My weaknesses/strengths
_____
_____

Coach advice
_____
_____
_____

Additional notes
_____
_____

PRACTICE

From Monday _____ to Friday _____ How many times __
                          Date
                next game _____ How many times __
                          Date

1st practice was: Very easy ☐ Easy ☐ Average ☐ Hard ☐ Very hard ☐
2nd practice was: Very easy ☐ Easy ☐ Average ☐ Hard ☐ Very hard ☐
3rd practice was: Very easy ☐ Easy ☐ Average ☐ Hard ☐ Very hard ☐

1st practice: 🙂 😐 🙁   2nd practice: 🙂 😐 🙁   3rd practice: 🙂 😐 🙁

Coach focused on
_____
_____
_____

I focused on
_____
_____

What I'v learnt
_____
_____

My weaknesses/strengths
_____
_____

Coach advice
_____
_____
_____

Additional notes
_____
_____

PRACTICE

From Monday _____ to < Friday _____ How many times ____
                Date   next game _____ How many times ____
                                       Date

1st practice was: Very easy ☐ Easy ☐ Average ☐ Hard ☐ Very hard ☐
2nd practice was: Very easy ☐ Easy ☐ Average ☐ Hard ☐ Very hard ☐
3rd practice was: Very easy ☐ Easy ☐ Average ☐ Hard ☐ Very hard ☐

1st practice: ☺ 😐 ☹   2nd practice: ☺ 😐 ☹   3rd practice: ☺ 😐 ☹

Coach focused on _____
_____
_____
_____

I focused on _____
_____
_____

What I'v learnt _____
_____
_____

My weaknesses/strengths _____
_____
_____

Coach advice _____
_____
_____

Additional notes _____
_____
_____

PRACTICE

From Monday _____ to < Friday _____   How many times ___
          Date   next game _____   How many times ___
                          Date   Date

1st practice was: Very easy ☐   Easy ☐   Average ☐   Hard ☐   Very hard ☐

2nd practice was: Very easy ☐   Easy ☐   Average ☐   Hard ☐   Very hard ☐

3rd practice was: Very easy ☐   Easy ☐   Average ☐   Hard ☐   Very hard ☐

1st practice: 🙂 😐 🙁   2nd practice: 🙂 😐 🙁   3rd practice: 🙂 😐 🙁

Coach focused on _____
_____
_____
_____

I focused on _____
_____
_____

What I'v learnt _____
_____
_____

My weaknesses/strengths _____
_____
_____

Coach advice _____
_____
_____
_____

Additional notes _____
_____
_____

PRACTICE

From Monday _____ to ⟨ Friday _____ How many times ___
                          Date
                          next game _____ How many times ___
                          Date

1ˢᵗ practice was: Very easy ☐ Easy ☐ Average ☐ Hard ☐ Very hard ☐

2ⁿᵈ practice was: Very easy ☐ Easy ☐ Average ☐ Hard ☐ Very hard ☐

3ʳᵈ practice was: Very easy ☐ Easy ☐ Average ☐ Hard ☐ Very hard ☐

1ˢᵗ practice: ☺ 😐 ☹   2ⁿᵈ practice: ☺ 😐 ☹   3ʳᵈ practice: ☺ 😐 ☹

Coach focused on
_____
_____
_____
_____

I focused on
_____
_____
_____
_____

What I'v learnt
_____
_____
_____
_____

My weaknesses/strengths
_____
_____
_____

Coach advice
_____
_____
_____
_____

Additional notes
_____
_____
_____

PRACTICE

From Monday _____ to Friday _____ How many times ___
                    Date   Date
               next game _____ How many times ___
                                  Date

1st practice was: Very easy ☐ Easy ☐ Average ☐ Hard ☐ Very hard ☐

2nd practice was: Very easy ☐ Easy ☐ Average ☐ Hard ☐ Very hard ☐

3rd practice was: Very easy ☐ Easy ☐ Average ☐ Hard ☐ Very hard ☐

1st practice: 🙂 😐 ☹️   2nd practice: 🙂 😐 ☹️   3rd practice: 🙂 😐 ☹️

Coach focused on
_____
_____
_____
_____

I focused on
_____
_____
_____

What I'v learnt
_____
_____
_____

My weaknesses/strengths
_____
_____
_____

Coach advice
_____
_____
_____

Additional notes
_____
_____
_____

GAME DAY

Date _____   Tournament ☐

Against _____ Time _____

Score - W D L _____   Home ☐ Away ☐

Position _____   Mood before match: ☺ 😐 ☹

Match was: Very easy ☐   Easy ☐   Average ☐   Hard ☐   Very hard ☐

Evaluation of my:

- warm up _____

_____

  - speed _____

_____

  - explosiveness & efficiency _____

_____

  - field position _____

_____

- finishing drives _____

_____

  - turnovers _____

_____

Good parts of my play were _____

_____

_____

What I could do better _____

_____

_____

I rate my performance today as_____

What I want to improve upon in practice _____

_____

_____

PRACTICE

From Monday _____ to < Friday _____   How many times ___
              Date   Date
                               next game _____   How many times ___
                                         Date

1st practice was: Very easy ☐ Easy ☐ Average ☐ Hard ☐ Very hard ☐

2nd practice was: Very easy ☐ Easy ☐ Average ☐ Hard ☐ Very hard ☐

3rd practice was: Very easy ☐ Easy ☐ Average ☐ Hard ☐ Very hard ☐

1st practice: 🙂 😐 🙁   2nd practice: 🙂 😐 🙁   3rd practice: 🙂 😐 🙁

Coach focused on
_____
_____
_____

I focused on
_____
_____
_____

What I'v learnt
_____
_____
_____

My weaknesses/strengths
_____
_____
_____

Coach advice
_____
_____
_____

Additional notes
_____
_____
_____

PRACTICE

From Monday _____ to ⟨ Friday _____ How many times ___
                Date   next game _____ How many times ___
                                      Date

1st practice was: Very easy ☐ Easy ☐ Average ☐ Hard ☐ Very hard ☐
2nd practice was: Very easy ☐ Easy ☐ Average ☐ Hard ☐ Very hard ☐
3rd practice was: Very easy ☐ Easy ☐ Average ☐ Hard ☐ Very hard ☐

1st practice: 🙂 😐 🙁   2nd practice: 🙂 😐 🙁   3rd practice: 🙂 😐 🙁

Coach focused on
_____
_____
_____

I focused on
_____
_____
_____

What I'v learnt
_____
_____
_____

My weaknesses/strengths
_____
_____
_____

Coach advice
_____
_____
_____

Additional notes
_____
_____
_____

PRACTICE

From Monday _____ to ⟨ Friday _____   How many times ___
Date   next game _____   How many times ___
                                    Date   Date

1st practice was: Very easy ☐   Easy ☐   Average ☐   Hard ☐   Very hard ☐
2nd practice was: Very easy ☐   Easy ☐   Average ☐   Hard ☐   Very hard ☐
3rd practice was: Very easy ☐   Easy ☐   Average ☐   Hard ☐   Very hard ☐

1st practice: 🙂😐🙁   2nd practice: 🙂😐🙁   3rd practice: 🙂😐🙁

Coach focused on
_____
_____
_____

I focused on
_____
_____

What I'v learnt
_____
_____

My weaknesses/strengths
_____
_____

Coach advice
_____
_____
_____

Additional notes
_____
_____

PRACTICE

From Monday _____ to ⟨Friday _____ How many times ____
                Date   Date
                        next game _____ How many times ____
                                   Date

1st practice was: Very easy ☐ Easy ☐ Average ☐ Hard ☐ Very hard ☐
2nd practice was: Very easy ☐ Easy ☐ Average ☐ Hard ☐ Very hard ☐
3rd practice was: Very easy ☐ Easy ☐ Average ☐ Hard ☐ Very hard ☐

1st practice: ☺ 😐 ☹   2nd practice: ☺ 😐 ☹   3rd practice: ☺ 😐 ☹

Coach focused on
_____
_____
_____
_____

I focused on
_____
_____
_____

What I'v learnt
_____
_____
_____

My weaknesses/strengths
_____
_____
_____

Coach advice
_____
_____
_____

Additional notes
_____
_____
_____

PRACTICE

From Monday _____ to ⟨ Friday _____   How many times ___
                Date   Date
                        next game _____   How many times ___
                                  Date

1st practice was: Very easy ☐ Easy ☐ Average ☐ Hard ☐ Very hard ☐

2nd practice was: Very easy ☐ Easy ☐ Average ☐ Hard ☐ Very hard ☐

3rd practice was: Very easy ☐ Easy ☐ Average ☐ Hard ☐ Very hard ☐

1st practice: ☺ 😐 ☹   2nd practice: ☺ 😐 ☹   3rd practice: ☺ 😐 ☹

Coach focused on
_____
_____
_____

I focused on
_____
_____
_____

What I'v learnt
_____
_____
_____

My weaknesses/strengths
_____
_____
_____

Coach advice
_____
_____
_____

Additional notes
_____
_____
_____

PRACTICE

From Monday _____ to < Friday _____ How many times ___
                Date   next game _____ How many times ___
                                      Date

1st practice was: Very easy ☐ Easy ☐ Average ☐ Hard ☐ Very hard ☐
2nd practice was: Very easy ☐ Easy ☐ Average ☐ Hard ☐ Very hard ☐
3rd practice was: Very easy ☐ Easy ☐ Average ☐ Hard ☐ Very hard ☐

1st practice: ☺ 😐 ☹   2nd practice: ☺ 😐 ☹   3rd practice: ☺ 😐 ☹

Coach focused on _____
_____
_____
_____

I focused on _____
_____
_____

What I'v learnt _____
_____
_____

My weaknesses/strengths _____
_____
_____

Coach advice _____
_____
_____

Additional notes _____
_____
_____

PRACTICE

From Monday _____ to Friday _____ How many times ___
                         Date   Date
                 next game _____ How many times ___
                              Date

1st practice was: Very easy ☐ Easy ☐ Average ☐ Hard ☐ Very hard ☐

2nd practice was: Very easy ☐ Easy ☐ Average ☐ Hard ☐ Very hard ☐

3rd practice was: Very easy ☐ Easy ☐ Average ☐ Hard ☐ Very hard ☐

1st practice: ☺ 😐 ☹   2nd practice: ☺ 😐 ☹   3rd practice: ☺ 😐 ☹

Coach focused on _____
_____
_____
_____

I focused on _____
_____
_____
_____

What I'v learnt _____
_____
_____
_____

My weaknesses/strengths _____
_____
_____

Coach advice _____
_____
_____
_____

Additional notes _____
_____
_____

PRACTICE

From Monday _____ to < Friday _____ How many times ___
Date   Date
                  next game _____ How many times ___
                              Date

1st practice was: Very easy ☐ Easy ☐ Average ☐ Hard ☐ Very hard ☐

2nd practice was: Very easy ☐ Easy ☐ Average ☐ Hard ☐ Very hard ☐

3rd practice was: Very easy ☐ Easy ☐ Average ☐ Hard ☐ Very hard ☐

1st practice: 🙂 😐 🙁 2nd practice: 🙂 😐 🙁 3rd practice: 🙂 😐 🙁

Coach focused on _____

_____

_____

_____

I focused on _____

_____

_____

What I'v learnt _____

_____

_____

My weaknesses/strengths _____

_____

_____

Coach advice _____

_____

_____

Additional notes _____

_____

_____

PRACTICE

From Monday _____ to Friday _____ How many times ___
                        Date   Date
                   next game _____ How many times ___
                                Date

1st practice was: Very easy ☐ Easy ☐ Average ☐ Hard ☐ Very hard ☐

2nd practice was: Very easy ☐ Easy ☐ Average ☐ Hard ☐ Very hard ☐

3rd practice was: Very easy ☐ Easy ☐ Average ☐ Hard ☐ Very hard ☐

1st practice: 🙂 😐 🙁   2nd practice: 🙂 😐 🙁   3rd practice: 🙂 😐 🙁

Coach focused on
_____
_____
_____

I focused on
_____
_____
_____

What I'v learnt
_____
_____
_____

My weaknesses/strengths
_____
_____
_____

Coach advice
_____
_____
_____
_____

Additional notes
_____
_____
_____

PRACTICE

From Monday _____ to < Friday _____   How many times ___
                           Date
                           next game _____   How many times ___
                                         Date

1st practice was: Very easy ☐ Easy ☐ Average ☐ Hard ☐ Very hard ☐
2nd practice was: Very easy ☐ Easy ☐ Average ☐ Hard ☐ Very hard ☐
3rd practice was: Very easy ☐ Easy ☐ Average ☐ Hard ☐ Very hard ☐

1st practice: 😊 😐 ☹   2nd practice: 😊 😐 ☹   3rd practice: 😊 😐 ☹

Coach focused on _____
_____
_____

I focused on _____
_____
_____

What I'v learnt _____
_____
_____

My weaknesses/strengths _____
_____
_____

Coach advice _____
_____
_____

Additional notes _____
_____
_____

PRACTICE

From Monday _____ to ⟨Friday _____ How many times ___
                Date   Date
             to ⟨next game _____ How many times ___
                                        Date

1st practice was: Very easy ☐ Easy ☐ Average ☐ Hard ☐ Very hard ☐
2nd practice was: Very easy ☐ Easy ☐ Average ☐ Hard ☐ Very hard ☐
3rd practice was: Very easy ☐ Easy ☐ Average ☐ Hard ☐ Very hard ☐

1st practice: ☺ 😐 ☹   2nd practice: ☺ 😐 ☹   3rd practice: ☺ 😐 ☹

Coach focused on
_____
_____
_____

I focused on
_____
_____
_____

What I'v learnt
_____
_____
_____

My weaknesses/strengths
_____
_____
_____

Coach advice
_____
_____
_____

Additional notes
_____
_____

GAME DAY

Date 3-25-23

Tournament ☐

Against TPT

Time 10:15 am

Score - W D L 15-1

Home ☐ Away ☑

Position _____

Mood before match: ☺ 😐 ☹

Match was: Very easy ☐ Easy ☐ Average ☑ Hard ☐ Very hard ☐

Evaluation of my:

- warm up running

- speed 15

- explosiveness & efficiency yes

- field position CB

- finishing drives TIP and Int

- turnovers 3

Good parts of my play were Did Not giv them they ball

What I could do better Defence

I rate my performance today as 1-10= 7

What I want to improve upon in practice catching

GAME DAY

Date _____   Tournament ☐

Against _____ Time _____

Score - W D L _____   Home☐ Away☐

Position _____   Mood before match: ☺ 😐 ☹

Match was: Very easy☐   Easy☐   Average☐   Hard☐   Very hard☐

Evaluation of my:

- warm up _____

_____

- speed _____

_____

- explosiveness & efficiency _____

_____

- field position _____

_____

- finishing drives _____

_____

- turnovers _____

_____

Good parts of my play were _____

_____

_____

What I could do better _____

_____

_____

I rate my performance today as_____

What I want to improve upon in practice _____

_____

GAME DAY

Date _____   Tournament ☐

Against _____ Time _____

Score - W D L _____   Home ☐ Away ☐

Position _____   Mood before match: ☺ 😐 ☹

Match was: Very easy ☐   Easy ☐   Average ☐   Hard ☐   Very hard ☐

Evaluation of my:

- warm up _____

_____

- speed _____

_____

- explosiveness & efficiency _____

_____

- field position _____

_____

- finishing drives _____

_____

- turnovers _____

_____

Good parts of my play were _____

_____

What I could do better _____

_____

_____

I rate my performance today as_____

What I want to improve upon in practice _____

_____

GAME DAY

Date _____   Tournament ☐

Against _____ Time _____

Score - W D L _____ Home☐ Away☐

Position _____ Mood before match: ☺ 😐 ☹

Match was: Very easy☐   Easy☐   Average☐   Hard☐   Very hard☐

Evaluation of my:

- warm up _____

_____

- speed _____

_____

- explosiveness & efficiency _____

_____

- field position _____

_____

- finishing drives _____

_____

- turnovers _____

_____

Good parts of my play were _____

_____

_____

What I could do better _____

_____

_____

I rate my performance today as_____

What I want to improve upon in practice _____

_____

_____

GAME DAY

Date _____ Tournament ☐

Against _____ Time _____

Score - W D L _____ Home ☐ Away ☐

Position _____ Mood before match: ☺ 😐 ☹

Match was: Very easy ☐ Easy ☐ Average ☐ Hard ☐ Very hard ☐

Evaluation of my:

- warm up _____

_____

- speed _____

_____

- explosiveness & efficiency _____

_____

- field position _____

_____

- finishing drives _____

_____

- turnovers _____

_____

Good parts of my play were _____

_____

_____

What I could do better _____

_____

_____

I rate my performance today as_____

What I want to improve upon in practice _____

_____

_____

GAME DAY

Date _____   Tournament ☐

Against _____ Time _____

Score - W D L _____ Home ☐ Away ☐

Position _____ Mood before match: ☺ 😐 ☹

Match was: Very easy ☐   Easy ☐   Average ☐   Hard ☐   Very hard ☐

Evaluation of my:

- warm up _____

_____

- speed _____

_____

- explosiveness & efficiency _____

_____

- field position _____

_____

- finishing drives _____

_____

- turnovers _____

_____

Good parts of my play were _____

_____

_____

What I could do better _____

_____

_____

I rate my performance today as_____

What I want to improve upon in practice _____

_____

_____

GAME DAY

Date _____ Tournament ☐

Against _____ Time _____

Score - W D L _____ Home ☐ Away ☐

Position _____ Mood before match: ☺ ☐ ☹

Match was: Very easy ☐ Easy ☐ Average ☐ Hard ☐ Very hard ☐

Evaluation of my:

- warm up _____

_____

- speed _____

_____

- explosiveness & efficiency _____

_____

- field position _____

_____

- finishing drives _____

_____

- turnovers _____

_____

Good parts of my play were _____

_____

_____

What I could do better _____

_____

_____

I rate my performance today as_____

What I want to improve upon in practice _____

_____

_____

GAME DAY

Date _____   Tournament ☐

Against _____ Time _____

Score - W D L _____   Home☐ Away☐

Position _____   Mood before match: ☺ 😐 ☹

Match was: Very easy☐   Easy☐   Average☐   Hard☐   Very hard☐

Evaluation of my:

   - warm up _____

_____

   - speed _____

_____

   - explosiveness & efficiency _____

_____

   - field position _____

_____

   - finishing drives _____

_____

   - turnovers _____

_____

Good parts of my play were _____

_____

_____

What I could do better _____

_____

_____

I rate my performance today as_____

What I want to improve upon in practice _____

_____

_____

GAME DAY

Date _____   Tournament ☐

Against _____ Time _____

Score - W D L _____   Home ☐ Away ☐

Position _____   Mood before match: ☺ 😐 ☹

Match was: Very easy ☐   Easy ☐   Average ☐   Hard ☐   Very hard ☐

Evaluation of my:

- warm up _____

_____

- speed _____

_____

- explosiveness & efficiency _____

_____

- field position _____

_____

- finishing drives _____

_____

- turnovers _____

_____

Good parts of my play were _____

_____

_____

What I could do better _____

_____

_____

I rate my performance today as_____

What I want to improve upon in practice _____

_____

GAME DAY

Date _____ Tournament ☐

Against _____ Time _____

Score - W D L _____ Home ☐ Away ☐

Position _____ Mood before match: ☺ 😐 ☹

Match was: Very easy ☐   Easy ☐   Average ☐   Hard ☐   Very hard ☐

Evaluation of my:

- warm up _____

_____

- speed _____

_____

- explosiveness & efficiency _____

_____

- field position _____

_____

- finishing drives _____

_____

- turnovers _____

_____

Good parts of my play were _____

_____

What I could do better _____

_____

_____

I rate my performance today as _____

What I want to improve upon in practice _____

_____

_____

GAME DAY

Date _____ Tournament ☐

Against _____ Time _____

Score - W D L _____ Home ☐ Away ☐

Position _____ Mood before match: 😊 😐 ☹️

Match was: Very easy ☐ Easy ☐ Average ☐ Hard ☐ Very hard ☐

Evaluation of my:

- warm up _____

_____

- speed _____

_____

- explosiveness & efficiency _____

_____

- field position _____

_____

- finishing drives _____

_____

- turnovers _____

_____

Good parts of my play were _____

_____

_____

What I could do better _____

_____

_____

I rate my performance today as_____

What I want to improve upon in practice _____

_____

_____

GAME DAY

Date _____   Tournament ☐

Against _____ Time _____

Score - W D L _____   Home ☐ Away ☐

Position _____   Mood before match: ☺ 😐 ☹

Match was: Very easy ☐   Easy ☐   Average ☐   Hard ☐   Very hard ☐

Evaluation of my:

- warm up _____
_____

- speed _____
_____

- explosiveness & efficiency _____
_____

- field position _____
_____

- finishing drives _____
_____

- turnovers _____
_____

Good parts of my play were _____
_____
_____

What I could do better _____
_____
_____

I rate my performance today as_____

What I want to improve upon in practice _____
_____
_____

GAME DAY

Date _____   Tournament ☐

Against _____ Time _____

Score - W D L _____   Home ☐ Away ☐

Position _____   Mood before match: ☺ ☺ ☹

Match was: Very easy ☐   Easy ☐   Average ☐   Hard ☐   Very hard ☐

Evaluation of my:

- warm up _____

_____

- speed _____

_____

- explosiveness & efficiency _____

_____

- field position _____

_____

- finishing drives _____

_____

- turnovers _____

_____

Good parts of my play were _____

_____

_____

What I could do better _____

_____

_____

I rate my performance today as_____

What I want to improve upon in practice _____

_____

_____

GAME DAY

Date _____   Tournament ☐

Against _____ Time _____

Score - W D L _____   Home ☐ Away ☐

Position _____   Mood before match: 😊 😐 ☹️

Match was: Very easy ☐   Easy ☐   Average ☐   Hard ☐   Very hard ☐

Evaluation of my:

- warm up _____

_____

- speed _____

_____

- explosiveness & efficiency _____

_____

- field position _____

_____

- finishing drives _____

_____

- turnovers _____

_____

Good parts of my play were _____

_____

_____

What I could do better _____

_____

_____

I rate my performance today as_____

What I want to improve upon in practice _____

_____

GAME DAY

Date _____   Tournament ☐

Against _____ Time _____

Score - W D L _____   Home ☐ Away ☐

Position _____   Mood before match: 🙂 😐 ☹️

Match was: Very easy ☐   Easy ☐   Average ☐   Hard ☐   Very hard ☐

Evaluation of my:

- warm up _____

_____

- speed _____

_____

- explosiveness & efficiency _____

_____

- field position _____

_____

- finishing drives _____

_____

- turnovers _____

_____

Good parts of my play were _____

_____

_____

What I could do better _____

_____

_____

I rate my performance today as_____

What I want to improve upon in practice _____

_____

_____

GAME DAY

Date _____   Tournament ☐

Against _____ Time _____
Score - W D L _____   Home ☐ Away ☐
Position _____   Mood before match: ☺ 😐 ☹
Match was: Very easy ☐   Easy ☐   Average ☐   Hard ☐   Very hard ☐

Evaluation of my:

- warm up _____

_____

- speed _____

_____

- explosiveness & efficiency _____

_____

- field position _____

_____

- finishing drives _____

_____

- turnovers _____

_____

Good parts of my play were _____

_____

_____

What I could do better _____

_____

_____

I rate my performance today as_____

What I want to improve upon in practice _____

_____

_____

GAME DAY

Date _____

Tournament ☐

Against _____ Time _____

Score - W D L _____ Home ☐ Away ☐

Position _____ Mood before match: 😊 😐 ☹️

Match was: Very easy ☐ Easy ☐ Average ☐ Hard ☐ Very hard ☐

Evaluation of my:

- warm up _____

_____

- speed _____

_____

- explosiveness & efficiency _____

_____

- field position _____

_____

- finishing drives _____

_____

- turnovers _____

_____

Good parts of my play were _____

_____

_____

What I could do better _____

_____

_____

I rate my performance today as_____

What I want to improve upon in practice _____

_____

_____

GAME DAY

Date _____   Tournament ☐

Against _____ Time _____

Score - W D L _____   Home ☐ Away ☐

Position _____   Mood before match: ☺ ☒ ☹

Match was: Very easy ☐   Easy ☐   Average ☐   Hard ☐   Very hard ☐

Evaluation of my:

   - warm up _____

_____

   - speed _____

_____

   - explosiveness & efficiency _____

_____

   - field position _____

_____

   - finishing drives _____

_____

   - turnovers _____

_____

Good parts of my play were _____

_____

_____

What I could do better _____

_____

_____

I rate my performance today as_____

What I want to improve upon in practice _____

_____

_____

GAME DAY

Date _____   Tournament ☐

Against _____ Time _____

Score - W D L _____   Home ☐ Away ☐

Position _____   Mood before match: ☺ 😐 ☹

Match was: Very easy ☐   Easy ☐   Average ☐   Hard ☐   Very hard ☐

Evaluation of my:

- warm up _____

_____

- speed _____

_____

- explosiveness & efficiency _____

_____

- field position _____

_____

- finishing drives _____

_____

- turnovers _____

_____

Good parts of my play were _____

_____

_____

What I could do better _____

_____

_____

I rate my performance today as_____

What I want to improve upon in practice _____

_____

GAME DAY

Date _____ **Tournament** ☐

Against _____ Time _____

Score - W D L _____ Home ☐ Away ☐

Position _____ Mood before match: ☺ 😐 ☹

Match was: Very easy ☐ Easy ☐ Average ☐ Hard ☐ Very hard ☐

Evaluation of my:

- warm up _____

_____

- speed _____

_____

- explosiveness & efficiency _____

_____

- field position _____

_____

- finishing drives _____

_____

- turnovers _____

_____

Good parts of my play were _____

_____

_____

What I could do better _____

_____

_____

I rate my performance today as_____

What I want to improve upon in practice _____

_____

GAME DAY

Date _____   Tournament ☐

Against _____ Time _____

Score - W D L _____ Home ☐ Away ☐

Position _____ Mood before match: ☺ 😐 ☹

Match was: Very easy ☐ Easy ☐ Average ☐ Hard ☐ Very hard ☐

Evaluation of my:

- warm up _____
_____

- speed _____
_____

- explosiveness & efficiency _____
_____

- field position _____
_____

- finishing drives _____
_____

- turnovers _____
_____

Good parts of my play were _____
_____
_____

What I could do better _____
_____
_____

I rate my performance today as _____

What I want to improve upon in practice _____
_____

GAME DAY

Date _____ **GAME DAY** Tournament ☐

Against _____ Time _____

Score - W D L _____ Home☐ Away☐

Position _____ Mood before match: ☺ 😐 ☹

Match was: Very easy☐   Easy☐   Average☐   Hard☐   Very hard☐

Evaluation of my:

- warm up _____

_____

- speed _____

_____

- explosiveness & efficiency _____

_____

- field position _____

_____

- finishing drives _____

_____

- turnovers _____

_____

Good parts of my play were _____

_____

_____

What I could do better _____

_____

_____

I rate my performance today as_____

What I want to improve upon in practice _____

_____

GAME DAY

Date _____   Tournament ☐

Against _____ Time _____
Score - W D L _____   Home☐ Away☐

Position _____   Mood before match: 🙂 😐 🙁

Match was: Very easy☐ Easy☐ Average☐ Hard☐ Very hard☐

Evaluation of my:

- warm up _____

_____

- speed _____

_____

- explosiveness & efficiency _____

_____

- field position _____

_____

- finishing drives _____

_____

- turnovers _____

_____

Good parts of my play were _____

_____

_____

What I could do better

_____

_____

_____

I rate my performance today as_____

What I want to improve upon in practice _____

_____

_____

GAME DAY

Date _____ Tournament ☐

Against _____ Time _____

Score - W D L _____ Home ☐ Away ☐

Position _____ Mood before match: ☺ 😐 ☹

Match was: Very easy ☐ Easy ☐ Average ☐ Hard ☐ Very hard ☐

Evaluation of my:

- warm up _____

_____

- speed _____

_____

- explosiveness & efficiency _____

_____

- field position _____

_____

- finishing drives _____

_____

- turnovers _____

_____

Good parts of my play were _____

_____

_____

What I could do better _____

_____

_____

I rate my performance today as_____

What I want to improve upon in practice _____

_____

GAME DAY

Date _____ Tournament ☐

Against _____ Time _____

Score - W D L _____ Home ☐ Away ☐

Position _____ Mood before match: ☺ 😐 ☹

Match was: Very easy ☐   Easy ☐   Average ☐   Hard ☐   Very hard ☐

Evaluation of my:

- warm up _____

_____

  - speed _____

_____

- explosiveness & efficiency _____

_____

  - field position _____

_____

- finishing drives _____

_____

  - turnovers _____

_____

Good parts of my play were _____

_____

_____

What I could do better _____

_____

_____

I rate my performance today as_____

What I want to improve upon in practice _____

_____

_____

GAME DAY

Date _____

Tournament ☐

Against _____ Time _____

Score - W D L _____ Home ☐ Away ☐

Position _____ Mood before match: ☺ 😐 ☹

Match was: Very easy ☐   Easy ☐   Average ☐   Hard ☐   Very hard ☐

Evaluation of my:

- warm up _____

_____

- speed _____

_____

- explosiveness & efficiency _____

_____

- field position _____

_____

- finishing drives _____

_____

- turnovers _____

_____

Good parts of my play were _____

_____

_____

What I could do better _____

_____

_____

I rate my performance today as_____

What I want to improve upon in practice _____

_____

GAME DAY

Date _____   Tournament ☐

Against _____ Time _____

Score - W D L _____   Home ☐ Away ☐

Position _____   Mood before match: ☺ 😐 ☹

Match was: Very easy ☐   Easy ☐   Average ☐   Hard ☐   Very hard ☐

Evaluation of my:

- warm up _____

_____

- speed _____

_____

- explosiveness & efficiency _____

_____

- field position _____

_____

- finishing drives _____

_____

- turnovers _____

_____

Good parts of my play were _____

_____

_____

What I could do better _____

_____

_____

I rate my performance today as_____

What I want to improve upon in practice _____

_____

_____

GAME DAY

Date _____   Tournament ☐

Against _____ Time _____

Score - W D L _____   Home ☐ Away ☐

Position _____   Mood before match: ☺ 😐 ☹

Match was: Very easy ☐   Easy ☐   Average ☐   Hard ☐   Very hard ☐

Evaluation of my:

- warm up _____

_____

- speed _____

_____

- explosiveness & efficiency _____

_____

- field position _____

_____

- finishing drives _____

_____

- turnovers _____

_____

Good parts of my play were _____

_____

_____

What I could do better _____

_____

_____

I rate my performance today as_____

What I want to improve upon in practice _____

_____

_____

GAME DAY

Date _____ **GAME DAY** Tournament ☐

Against _____ Time _____

Score - W D L _____ Home ☐ Away ☐

Position _____ Mood before match: ☺ 😐 ☹

Match was: Very easy ☐ Easy ☐ Average ☐ Hard ☐ Very hard ☐

Evaluation of my:

- warm up _____

_____

- speed _____

_____

- explosiveness & efficiency _____

_____

- field position _____

_____

- finishing drives _____

_____

- turnovers _____

_____

Good parts of my play were _____

_____

_____

What I could do better _____

_____

_____

I rate my performance today as_____

What I want to improve upon in practice _____

_____

_____

GAME DAY

Date _____

Tournament ☐

Against _____ Time _____

Score - W D L _____ Home ☐ Away ☐

Position _____ Mood before match: ☺ 😐 ☹

Match was: Very easy ☐   Easy ☐   Average ☐   Hard ☐   Very hard ☐

Evaluation of my:

- warm up _____

_____

- speed _____

_____

- explosiveness & efficiency _____

_____

- field position _____

_____

- finishing drives _____

_____

- turnovers _____

_____

Good parts of my play were _____

_____

_____

What I could do better _____

_____

_____

I rate my performance today as_____

What I want to improve upon in practice _____

_____

_____

GAME DAY

Date _____   Tournament ☐

Against _____ Time _____

Score - W D L _____   Home ☐ Away ☐

Position _____   Mood before match: ☺ 😐 ☹

Match was: Very easy ☐   Easy ☐   Average ☐   Hard ☐   Very hard ☐

Evaluation of my:

- warm up _____

_____

- speed _____

_____

- explosiveness & efficiency _____

_____

- field position _____

_____

- finishing drives _____

_____

- turnovers _____

_____

Good parts of my play were _____

_____

_____

What I could do better _____

_____

_____

I rate my performance today as_____

What I want to improve upon in practice _____

_____

_____

GAME DAY

Date _____ Tournament ☐

Against _____ Time _____

Score - W D L _____ Home ☐ Away ☐

Position _____ Mood before match: ☺ 😐 ☹

Match was: Very easy ☐ Easy ☐ Average ☐ Hard ☐ Very hard ☐

Evaluation of my:

- warm up _____

_____

- speed _____

_____

- explosiveness & efficiency _____

_____

- field position _____

_____

- finishing drives _____

_____

- turnovers _____

_____

Good parts of my play were _____

_____

_____

What I could do better _____

_____

_____

I rate my performance today as_____

What I want to improve upon in practice _____

_____

_____

GAME DAY

Date _____   Tournament ☐

Against _____ Time _____

Score - W D L _____ Home ☐ Away ☐

Position _____ Mood before match: 😊 😐 ☹️

Match was: Very easy ☐   Easy ☐   Average ☐   Hard ☐   Very hard ☐

Evaluation of my:

- warm up _____

_____

   - speed _____

_____

   - explosiveness & efficiency _____

_____

   - field position _____

_____

   - finishing drives _____

_____

   - turnovers _____

_____

Good parts of my play were _____

_____

_____

What I could do better _____

_____

_____

I rate my performance today as_____

What I want to improve upon in practice _____

_____

_____

GAME DAY

Date _____ Tournament ☐

Against _____ Time _____

Score - W D L _____ Home ☐ Away ☐

Position _____ Mood before match: 🙂 😐 🙁

Match was: Very easy ☐   Easy ☐   Average ☐   Hard ☐   Very hard ☐

Evaluation of my:

- warm up _____

_____

  - speed _____

_____

  - explosiveness & efficiency _____

_____

  - field position _____

_____

  - finishing drives _____

_____

  - turnovers _____

_____

Good parts of my play were _____

_____

_____

What I could do better _____

_____

_____

I rate my performance today as_____

What I want to improve upon in practice _____

_____

_____

GAME DAY

Date _____ **GAME DAY** Tournament ☐

Against _____ Time _____

Score - W D L _____ Home ☐ Away ☐

Position _____ Mood before match: ☺ 😐 ☹

Match was: Very easy ☐ Easy ☐ Average ☐ Hard ☐ Very hard ☐

Evaluation of my:

- warm up _____

_____

- speed _____

_____

- explosiveness & efficiency _____

_____

- field position _____

_____

- finishing drives _____

_____

- turnovers _____

_____

Good parts of my play were _____

_____

_____

What I could do better _____

_____

_____

I rate my performance today as_____

What I want to improve upon in practice _____

_____

_____

GAME DAY

Date _____ Tournament ☐

Against _____ Time _____

Score - W D L _____ Home☐ Away☐

Position _____ Mood before match: ☺ 😐 ☹

Match was: Very easy☐ Easy☐ Average☐ Hard☐ Very hard☐

Evaluation of my:

- warm up _____

_____

- speed _____

_____

- explosiveness & efficiency _____

_____

- field position _____

_____

- finishing drives _____

_____

- turnovers _____

_____

Good parts of my play were _____

_____

_____

What I could do better _____

_____

_____

I rate my performance today as_____

What I want to improve upon in practice _____

_____

_____

GAME DAY

Date _____   Tournament ☐

Against _____ Time _____

Score - W D L _____   Home ☐ Away ☐

Position _____   Mood before match: ☺ 😐 ☹

Match was: Very easy ☐ Easy ☐ Average ☐ Hard ☐ Very hard ☐

Evaluation of my:

- warm up _____

_____

- speed _____

_____

- explosiveness & efficiency _____

_____

- field position _____

_____

- finishing drives _____

_____

- turnovers _____

_____

Good parts of my play were _____

_____

_____

What I could do better _____

_____

_____

I rate my performance today as_____

What I want to improve upon in practice _____

_____

_____

GAME DAY

Date _____   Tournament ☐

Against _____ Time _____

Score - W D L _____   Home ☐ Away ☐

Position _____   Mood before match: 😊 😐 ☹️

Match was: Very easy ☐   Easy ☐   Average ☐   Hard ☐   Very hard ☐

Evaluation of my:

- warm up _____

_____

- speed _____

_____

- explosiveness & efficiency _____

_____

- field position _____

_____

- finishing drives _____

_____

- turnovers _____

_____

Good parts of my play were _____

_____

_____

What I could do better _____

_____

_____

I rate my performance today as_____

What I want to improve upon in practice ____

_____

_____

GAME DAY

Date _____   Tournament ☐

Against _____ Time _____

Score - W D L _____   Home ☐ Away ☐

Position _____   Mood before match: ☺ 😐 ☹

Match was: Very easy ☐   Easy ☐   Average ☐   Hard ☐   Very hard ☐

Evaluation of my:

- warm up _____

_____

- speed _____

_____

- explosiveness & efficiency _____

_____

- field position _____

_____

- finishing drives _____

_____

- turnovers _____

_____

Good parts of my play were _____

_____

What I could do better _____

_____

_____

I rate my performance today as_____

What I want to improve upon in practice _____

_____

_____

GAME DAY

Date _____   Tournament ☐

Against _____ Time _____

Score - W D L _____   Home ☐ Away ☐

Position _____   Mood before match: ☺ 😐 ☹

Match was: Very easy ☐   Easy ☐   Average ☐   Hard ☐   Very hard ☐

Evaluation of my:

- warm up _____
_____

- speed _____
_____

- explosiveness & efficiency _____
_____

- field position _____
_____

- finishing drives _____
_____

- turnovers _____
_____

Good parts of my play were _____
_____

What I could do better _____
_____
_____

I rate my performance today as_____

What I want to improve upon in practice _____
_____

GAME DAY

Date _____   Tournament ☐

Against _____ Time _____

Score - W D L _____   Home ☐ Away ☐

Position _____   Mood before match: ☺ 😐 ☹

Match was: Very easy ☐   Easy ☐   Average ☐   Hard ☐   Very hard ☐

Evaluation of my:

   - warm up _____

_____

   - speed _____

_____

   - explosiveness & efficiency _____

_____

   - field position _____

_____

   - finishing drives _____

_____

   - turnovers _____

_____

Good parts of my play were _____

_____

_____

What I could do better _____

_____

_____

I rate my performance today as_____

What I want to improve upon in practice _____

_____

GAME DAY

Date _____   Tournament ☐

Against _____ Time _____

Score - W D L _____   Home ☐ Away ☐

Position _____   Mood before match: ☺ 😐 ☹

Match was: Very easy ☐   Easy ☐   Average ☐   Hard ☐   Very hard ☐

Evaluation of my:

- warm up _____

_____

- speed _____

_____

- explosiveness & efficiency _____

_____

- field position _____

_____

- finishing drives _____

_____

- turnovers _____

_____

Good parts of my play were _____

_____

_____

What I could do better _____

_____

_____

I rate my performance today as_____

What I want to improve upon in practice _____

_____

_____

GAME DAY

Date _____   Tournament ☐

Against _____ Time _____

Score - W D L _____   Home ☐ Away ☐

Position _____   Mood before match: ☺ 😐 ☹

Match was: Very easy ☐   Easy ☐   Average ☐   Hard ☐   Very hard ☐

Evaluation of my:

- warm up _____

_____

- speed _____

_____

- explosiveness & efficiency _____

_____

- field position _____

_____

- finishing drives _____

_____

- turnovers _____

_____

Good parts of my play were _____

_____

_____

What I could do better _____

_____

_____

I rate my performance today as_____

What I want to improve upon in practice _____

_____

_____

GAME DAY

Date _____

Tournament ☐

Against _____ Time _____

Score - W D L _____ Home ☐ Away ☐

Position _____ Mood before match: ☺ 😐 ☹

Match was: Very easy ☐   Easy ☐   Average ☐   Hard ☐   Very hard ☐

Evaluation of my:

- warm up _____

_____

- speed _____

_____

- explosiveness & efficiency _____

_____

- field position _____

_____

- finishing drives _____

_____

- turnovers _____

_____

Good parts of my play were _____

_____

_____

What I could do better _____

_____

_____

I rate my performance today as_____

What I want to improve upon in practice _____

_____

_____

GAME DAY

Date _____

Tournament ☐

Against _____ Time _____

Score - W D L _____ Home ☐ Away ☐

Position _____ Mood before match: ☺ 😐 ☹

Match was: Very easy ☐ Easy ☐ Average ☐ Hard ☐ Very hard ☐

Evaluation of my:

- warm up _____

_____

- speed _____

_____

- explosiveness & efficiency _____

_____

- field position _____

_____

- finishing drives _____

_____

- turnovers _____

_____

Good parts of my play were _____

_____

_____

What I could do better _____

_____

_____

I rate my performance today as_____

What I want to improve upon in practice _____

_____

_____

GAME DAY

Date _____   Tournament ☐

Against _____ Time _____

Score - W D L _____   Home ☐ Away ☐

Position _____   Mood before match: ☺ 😐 ☹

Match was: Very easy ☐   Easy ☐   Average ☐   Hard ☐   Very hard ☐

Evaluation of my:

- warm up _____

_____

   - speed _____

_____

   - explosiveness & efficiency _____

_____

   - field position _____

_____

   - finishing drives _____

_____

   - turnovers _____

_____

Good parts of my play were _____

_____

_____

What I could do better _____

_____

_____

I rate my performance today as_____

What I want to improve upon in practice _____

_____

GAME DAY

Date _____   Tournament ☐

Against _____ Time _____

Score - W D L _____   Home ☐ Away ☐

Position _____   Mood before match: ☺ 😐 ☹

Match was: Very easy ☐   Easy ☐   Average ☐   Hard ☐   Very hard ☐

Evaluation of my:

- warm up _____

_____

- speed _____

_____

- explosiveness & efficiency _____

_____

- field position _____

_____

- finishing drives _____

_____

- turnovers _____

_____

Good parts of my play were _____

_____

_____

What I could do better _____

_____

_____

I rate my performance today as_____

What I want to improve upon in practice _____

_____

_____

GAME DAY

Date _____ Tournament ☐

Against _____ Time _____
Score - W D L _____ Home ☐ Away ☐
Position _____ Mood before match: ☺ 😐 ☹
Match was: Very easy ☐ Easy ☐ Average ☐ Hard ☐ Very hard ☐

Evaluation of my:

- warm up _____
_____

- speed _____
_____

- explosiveness & efficiency _____
_____

- field position _____
_____

- finishing drives _____
_____

- turnovers _____
_____

Good parts of my play were _____
_____
_____

What I could do better _____
_____
_____

I rate my performance today as_____
What I want to improve upon in practice _____
_____
_____

GAME DAY

Date _____ Tournament ☐

Against _____ Time _____

Score - W D L _____ Home ☐ Away ☐

Position _____ Mood before match: ☺ 😐 ☹

Match was: Very easy ☐ Easy ☐ Average ☐ Hard ☐ Very hard ☐

Evaluation of my:

- warm up _____

_____

- speed _____

_____

- explosiveness & efficiency _____

_____

- field position _____

_____

- finishing drives _____

_____

- turnovers _____

_____

Good parts of my play were _____

_____

_____

What I could do better

_____

_____

I rate my performance today as_____

What I want to improve upon in practice _____

_____

GAME DAY

Date _____ Tournament ☐

Against _____ Time _____

Score - W D L _____ Home ☐ Away ☐

Position _____ Mood before match: 🙂 😐 ☹️

Match was: Very easy ☐ Easy ☐ Average ☐ Hard ☐ Very hard ☐

Evaluation of my:

- warm up _____

_____

- speed _____

_____

- explosiveness & efficiency _____

_____

- field position _____

_____

- finishing drives _____

_____

- turnovers _____

_____

Good parts of my play were _____

_____

_____

What I could do better _____

_____

_____

I rate my performance today as_____

What I want to improve upon in practice _____

_____

GAME DAY

Date _____   Tournament ☐

Against _____ Time _____

Score - W D L _____   Home ☐ Away ☐

Position _____   Mood before match: ☺ ☺ ☹

Match was: Very easy ☐   Easy ☐   Average ☐   Hard ☐   Very hard ☐

Evaluation of my:

- warm up _____

_____

- speed _____

_____

- explosiveness & efficiency _____

_____

- field position _____

_____

- finishing drives _____

_____

- turnovers _____

_____

Good parts of my play were _____

_____

_____

What I could do better _____

_____

_____

I rate my performance today as_____

What I want to improve upon in practice _____

_____

_____

GAME DAY

Date _____   Tournament ☐

Against _____ Time _____

Score - W D L _____   Home☐ Away☐

Position _____ Mood before match: ☺ 😐 ☹

Match was: Very easy☐ Easy☐ Average☐ Hard☐ Very hard☐

Evaluation of my:

- warm up _____

_____

- speed _____

_____

- explosiveness & efficiency _____

_____

- field position _____

_____

- finishing drives _____

_____

- turnovers _____

_____

Good parts of my play were _____

_____

_____

What I could do better _____

_____

_____

I rate my performance today as_____

What I want to improve upon in practice _____

_____

_____

GAME DAY

Date _____ Tournament ☐

Against _____ Time _____

Score - W D L _____ Home ☐ Away ☐

Position _____ Mood before match: 🙂 😐 🙁

Match was: Very easy ☐   Easy ☐   Average ☐   Hard ☐   Very hard ☐

Evaluation of my:

- warm up _____

_____

- speed _____

_____

- explosiveness & efficiency _____

_____

- field position _____

_____

- finishing drives _____

_____

- turnovers _____

_____

Good parts of my play were _____

_____

_____

What I could do better _____

_____

_____

I rate my performance today as_____

What I want to improve upon in practice _____

_____

_____

GAME DAY

Date _____ Tournament ☐

Against _____ Time _____

Score - W D L _____ Home ☐ Away ☐

Position _____ Mood before match: ☺ 😐 ☹

Match was: Very easy ☐   Easy ☐   Average ☐   Hard ☐   Very hard ☐

Evaluation of my:

- warm up _____

_____

  - speed _____

_____

  - explosiveness & efficiency _____

_____

  - field position _____

_____

  - finishing drives _____

_____

  - turnovers _____

_____

Good parts of my play were _____

_____

_____

What I could do better _____

_____

_____

I rate my performance today as_____

What I want to improve upon in practice _____

_____

_____

GAME DAY

Date _____   Tournament ☐

Against _____ Time _____

Score - W D L _____   Home ☐ Away ☐

Position _____   Mood before match: 😊 😐 ☹️

Match was: Very easy ☐   Easy ☐   Average ☐   Hard ☐   Very hard ☐

Evaluation of my:

- warm up _____

_____

- speed _____

_____

- explosiveness & efficiency _____

_____

- field position _____

_____

- finishing drives _____

_____

- turnovers _____

_____

Good parts of my play were _____

_____

_____

What I could do better _____

_____

_____

I rate my performance today as_____

What I want to improve upon in practice _____

_____

GAME DAY

Date _____   Tournament ☐

Against _____ Time _____

Score - W D L _____   Home ☐ Away ☐

Position _____   Mood before match: ☺ 😐 ☹

Match was: Very easy ☐   Easy ☐   Average ☐   Hard ☐   Very hard ☐

Evaluation of my:

- warm up _____

_____

   - speed _____

_____

   - explosiveness & efficiency _____

_____

   - field position _____

_____

   - finishing drives _____

_____

   - turnovers _____

_____

Good parts of my play were _____

_____

_____

What I could do better _____

_____

_____

I rate my performance today as_____

What I want to improve upon in practice _____

_____

_____

GAME DAY

Date _____   Tournament ☐

Against _____ Time _____

Score - W D L _____   Home ☐ Away ☐

Position _____   Mood before match: ☺ 😐 ☹

Match was: Very easy ☐ Easy ☐ Average ☐ Hard ☐ Very hard ☐

Evaluation of my:

- warm up _____

_____

- speed _____

_____

- explosiveness & efficiency _____

_____

- field position _____

_____

- finishing drives _____

_____

- turnovers _____

_____

Good parts of my play were _____

_____

_____

What I could do better _____

_____

_____

I rate my performance today as _____

What I want to improve upon in practice _____

_____

_____

GAME DAY

Date _____ Tournament ☐

Against _____ Time _____

Score - W D L _____ Home ☐ Away ☐

Position _____ Mood before match: ☺ 😐 ☹

Match was: Very easy ☐ Easy ☐ Average ☐ Hard ☐ Very hard ☐

Evaluation of my:

- warm up _____

_____

- speed _____

_____

- explosiveness & efficiency _____

_____

- field position _____

_____

- finishing drives _____

_____

- turnovers _____

_____

Good parts of my play were _____

_____

_____

What I could do better _____

_____

_____

I rate my performance today as_____

What I want to improve upon in practice _____

_____

_____

GAME DAY

Date _____

Tournament ☐

Against _____ Time _____

Score - W D L _____ Home ☐ Away ☐

Position _____ Mood before match: ☺ 😐 ☹

Match was: Very easy ☐   Easy ☐   Average ☐   Hard ☐   Very hard ☐

Evaluation of my:

- warm up _____

_____

- speed _____

_____

- explosiveness & efficiency _____

_____

- field position _____

_____

- finishing drives _____

_____

- turnovers _____

_____

Good parts of my play were _____

_____

_____

What I could do better

_____

_____

I rate my performance today as_____

What I want to improve upon in practice _____

_____

GAME DAY

Date _____   Tournament ☐

Against _____ Time _____

Score - W D L _____   Home ☐ Away ☐

Position _____   Mood before match: ☺ 😐 ☹

Match was: Very easy ☐   Easy ☐   Average ☐   Hard ☐   Very hard ☐

Evaluation of my:

- warm up _____

_____

 - speed _____

_____

 - explosiveness & efficiency _____

_____

 - field position _____

_____

 - finishing drives _____

_____

 - turnovers _____

_____

Good parts of my play were _____

_____

_____

What I could do better _____

_____

_____

I rate my performance today as_____

What I want to improve upon in practice _____

_____

_____

Made in the USA
Las Vegas, NV
09 March 2023

68809399R00068